Coding for Kids C++

Basic Guide for Kids to Learn Commands and How to Write a Program

GoldInk Books

BEFORE YOU START READING, DOWNLOAD YOUR FREE DIGITAL ASSETS!

Be sure to visit the URL below on your computer or mobile device to access the free digital asset files that are included with your purchase of this book.

These digital assets will complement the material in the book and are referenced throughout the text.

DOWNLOAD YOURS HERE:

www.GoldInkBooks.com

GOLDINK BOOKS

GoldInk Books is a self-publishing company. We produce books in a range of genres with efficiency, speed and convenience of digital publishing. Our researchers and authors are dedicated to bring high-quality research to people all over the world. All of our books are available to read and download online. We use technology to make the book publishing sector more accountable. We are known for taking a serious and intellectual approach to different topics with popular appeal. To strengthen the pillars of knowledge, we want to put a book in everyone's hands and create an active network of digital creative communities.

© **Copyright 2021 by (GoldInk Books) - All rights reserved.**

This document is geared towards providing exact and reliable information in regard to the topic and issue covered. The publication is sold with the idea that the publisher is not required to render accounting, officially permitted, or otherwise, qualified services. If advice is necessary, legal or professional, a practiced individual in the profession should be ordered.

From a Declaration of Principles which was accepted and approved equally by a Committee of the American Bar Association and a Committee of Publishers and Associations.

In no way is it legal to reproduce, duplicate, or transmit any part of this document in either electronic means or in printed format. Recording of this publication is strictly prohibited and any storage of this document is not allowed unless with written permission from the publisher. All rights reserved.

The information provided herein is stated to be truthful and consistent, in that any liability, in terms of inattention or otherwise, by any usage or abuse of any policies, processes, or directions contained within is the solitary and utter responsibility of the recipient reader. Under no circumstances will any legal responsibility or blame be held against the publisher for any reparation, damages, or monetary loss due to the information herein, either directly or indirectly.

Respective author(s) own all copyrights not held by the publisher.

The information herein is offered for informational purposes solely and is universal as so. The presentation of the information is without a contract or any type of guarantee assurance.

The trademarks that are used are without any consent, and the publication of the trademark is without permission or backing by the trademark owner. All trademarks and brands within this book are for clarifying purposes only and are owned by the owners themselves, not affiliated with this document.

Table of Contents

INTRODUCTION 8

CHAPTER 1: GETTING STARTED WITH C++ 12

1.1 What is C++? 12

1.2 Five Basic Concepts of C++ 13

1.3 What is Code Editor and Its Installation? 16

1.4 C++ "Hello, World!" Program 22

CHAPTER 2: VARIABLES, DATA TYPE, AND OPERATOR IN C++ 26

2.1 Variables of C++ 26

2.2 Different Data Types in C++ 29

2.3 Operators in C++ 33

CHAPTER 3: STRINGS IN C++ 40

3.1 What is String? 40

CHAPTER 4: ARRAY IN C++ 46

4.1 Introduction to Array 46

4.2 Types of Arrays in C++ 48

4.3 Creating and Passing an Array 52

CHAPTER 5: C++ POINTERS 55

5.1 What are Pointers? 55

5.2 Declaring Pointers in C++ 57

CHAPTER 6: CONTROL STATEMENTS AND LOOPS..... 60

6.1 Statements and Flow Control...60

6.2 Selection Statements:..61

6.3 Iteration Statements (loops) 65

6.4 Jump Statements 71

CHAPTER 7: FUNCTION AND SCOPE OF VARIABLE.... 73

7.1 C++ Function..73

7.2 Types of Functions in C++ 75

7.3 Function Declaration and Definition 78

7.4 Scope of Variables 80

CHAPTER 8: CLASS AND OBJECTS IN C++ 84

8.1 C++ Class...84

8.2 C++ Object..88

8.3 Concepts of C++ Object-Oriented Programming..........................90

CONCLUSION 93

Introduction

Why should children be left behind when anyone can learn to code? Once, coding was only limited to computer engineers sitting silently typing away at endless lines of code. However, thanks to technological advancements, children can now enjoy it at their fingertips. The terms "mobile games," "smartphones," "tablets," and "computer games" are no longer jargon. Children are using high-tech gadgets for educational and entertaining purposes. They are mastering them much more quickly and efficiently than adults because young minds have a remarkable potential to explore and focus when utilized appropriately.

Programming is one of the most valuable abilities in today's world. Since most of the apps and websites are constructed on the foundation of programming, programming has become one of the most crucial skills to acquire in recent years. C++ is one of the most significant programming languages, but many students are unsure whether or not to begin with it.

C++ may be challenging for children since it appears to be a lot of Math, discouraging them from learning to code. However, once pupils grasp the basics of C++, there is no going back. You might be shocked to learn that the majority of great programmers began their careers with C++.

C++ is known for having a high learning curve, but if your children are encouraged to study it, it will benefit their programming careers greatly. C++ will assist your youngster in developing real-world problem-solving abilities while also providing a solid foundation in programming concepts. C++ can also aid in the development of strong programming habits, resulting in a clear and consistent writing style.

In this book, we will go over some fundamental C++ topics for youngsters. We will also go over the advantages and disadvantages of teaching youngsters C++.

Why C++?

C++ is a general-purpose computer language that is case-sensitive. It supports procedural, generic, and object-oriented programming. It is classified as a middle-level language since it has characteristics of both low and high-level languages.

Let's look at what C++ is used for so that we can understand the importance of this language.

What is the Purpose of C++?

C++ is a performance-oriented programming language that works with a wide range of programs and challenges. It concentrates on large-scale system programming. It aids in the development of 3D animation, web browsers such as Firefox Chrome, and other applications such as medical software, office software, and so on. It is also in Blizzard games, MRI scanners, and PDF technology, among other things.

We can create a variety of secure and robust applications using C programming, such as Window apps, Device Drivers, Embedded firmware, Client-server applications, and so on.

It is used to program the CPU's various functions using procedural programming. C++ is also used extensively in the development of video games. Not only this, but C++ is also used by search engines like Chrome, Mozilla, and Firefox. It is a very important programming language because of its vast range of applications.

About this Guide

This book will go over the fundamental concepts of C++. This manual has been designed to be a step-by-step, bit-by-bit guide to guarantee that you understand everything. To begin, you must understand the foundations of sentence formation, sometimes known as syntax. The following parts will walk you through important expressions, functions, and the construction of small programs in C++.

Furthermore, this book covers C++ choices, operators, arrays, logical data, classes, pointers, and strings, among other topics. I am glad that you have decided to read this book before digging deeper into C++. This guide will help you with.

- C++'s basic knowledge.
- Coding basics.
- How to Get Started with C++ Coding.
- How to Create C++ Projects?
- Basic and Intermediate Syntax in C++
- Unmistakable and irresistible traits of C++
- Numerous applications of C++

- C++ compilers, integrated development environments, and text editors.
- Data Types, Variables, and Operators.
- C++ expressions.
- OOP Concepts of C++
- In C++ programming, you will learn about module creation, exceptions, and arrays.
- C++ libraries are used to store data.

For Which Age Groups Is this Guide Appropriate?

This guide has been designed for new learners, particularly for 12 years old and up.

Furthermore, this guide is great for parents who want to teach their children C++ programming.

Important Recommendations

This book will be more beneficial if you try to code in and construct your applications while reading it.

In this book, we have discussed some of the most important C++ subjects. It is one of the most suitable coding languages for children to begin their programming careers. They can become coding geniuses by mastering C++. I hope this book would help you to learn C++ in a fun way.

Good luck with your studies!

Chapter 1: Getting Started with C++

Java, C++, Python, and C are the most often used languages. Instead of thinking about the problem in terms of business logic, these languages encourage the programmer to think about it in terms of computer programming and implementations. Despite the fact that it is old, C++ is still widely used today, which is a remarkable achievement in and of itself. C++ is still widely used, and the most well-known software is built on it.

This chapter talks about the fundamentals, advanced ideas, applications, and concepts of C++. It also discusses C++'s background and tools that are used to do C++. Then, you will learn to make your first program.

1.1 What is C++?

C++ is basically an OOP Language. OOP means object-oriented programming language developed by renowned computer scientist Bjorne Stroustrup as part of a C language family's growth. "See-pluss-pluss" is how C++ is pronounced. It is created in the form of a cross-platform enhancement to C that would provide developers more control on memory and system resources.

C++ is known as "C including Classes" because C++ adds OOPs techniques to the C basic programming language foundation, including the use of specified classes. C++ has shown to be a valuable language not just for computer programming but also for training novice programmers on how to use OOP.

However, it supports not only OOP but also functional and procedural programming.

C++ is popular today because of its remarkable portability and easiness, which allows programmers to simply design applications that operate on a variety of operating systems and platforms. Although it is a high-level language, C++ may be used to manipulate low-level data because of its strong relationship with many machine languages.

Short Background

Bjarne Stroustrup created C++ at the start of the 1980s at Bell Labs to combine the finest features of numerous existing languages. He sought to combine the speed of exciting BCPL, commonly a high level of Simula, and also the universality and combination of Dennis Ritchie's C in a single package. He drew on other languages like ML, Ada, and also ALGOL 68 to construct a general-purpose and well-structured language that can compile practically all programs of C without modifying their actual source code.

1.2 Five Basic Concepts of C++

1. Variables in C++

Variables are the fundamental building blocks of any programming language. A variable is nothing more than means to save data for later use. This value or data can be retrieved by referring to a "word" that describes the information. They can be used numerous times within the scope in which they were declared and defined once they have been declared and defined.

2. Control Structures in C++

The compiler reads the code line by line when a program executes (from top to bottom, and for the most part, left to right). This is known as "code flow. "When reading the code from beginning to end, it may come to a point when it must make a decision. The software may jump to a different area of the code depending on the decision. It may even cause the compiler to re-run a certain section or simply skip a section of code.

Consider this approach as if you were selecting from a variety of Guru99 courses. You make a decision, then click a link to skip a few pages. Similarly, a computer program has a set of strict rules that determine how the program is executed.

3. Data Structures in C++

Let's take a look at a list of courses (on any site) as an example! You most likely have a course schedule in front of you. But, what do you think they did with it? There may be a large number of courses, and different people sign up for different ones. Is each user's variable generated differently? Let's imagine we need to keep track of ten different courses.

Then There is the WRONG WAY:

We would define ten variables if we needed to hold ten courses. Right?

Wrong!!!

This is a terrible approach to try to store ten separate variables in the realm of programming. This is due to two key factors:

The enormous amount of text that will be required in your program. Sure, we only have ten classes right now, so it is not horrible, but what if we had 1,000? Consider how many times you would have to type it! Put it out of your mind!

Manual code adjustments would be required to add another course. Variable course11 would have been created. This is completely insane!

So, what is the RIGHT WAY to do things?

Data structures are used to store them.

Using a data structure, you may avoid having to construct thousands of variables. C++ has a large number of built-in data structures. Arrays, which will be introduced later, are the most commonly utilized data structure.

4. Syntax in C++

Syntax is a set of rules for how words, expressions, and symbols are organized. This is due to the fact that an email address has a well-defined syntax. You will need a mixture of letters and numbers, possibly with underscores (_) or periods (.) in between, and at the rate (@) sign, and a website domain (company.com).

As a result, the grammar of a programming language is very similar. They are a set of well-defined rules that allow you to develop a working piece of software.

You will get errors if you do not follow the rules of a programming language or grammar.

5. Tools for C++

A tool (typically a tangible device) helps you do a task quickly in the real world. This holds true in the programming world as well. A programming tool is a piece of software that, when combined with code, allows you to program more quickly.

Across all programming languages, there are probably tens of thousands, if not millions, of different tools. Many people believe that an IDE, or Integrated Development Environment, is the most important tool. An IDE is a piece of software that makes coding much easier. IDEs keep your files and folders organized and present them in a neat and tidy manner.

1.3 What is Code Editor and Its Installation?

What exactly is IDE?

The IDE, or Integrated Development Environment, is a digital environment used to build games, software, and hardware that integrates everything from debugging to compiling. Some C++ IDEs only support a single language, such as IDLE, which only supports Python. On the other hand, Apple's Xcode supports a variety of languages, including C, C++, Java, and others.

This chapter will offer you clear and basic explanations of each C++ IDE so you can pick the one that is right for you. You may also try out a few other IDEs on your PC to discover which one works best for you.

Dev-C++

Features of this IDE:

- GCC-based compilers, such as Cygwin, MinGW, and others, are supported by Dev-C++. If we already have a compiler on our PC, we may either install a Dev-C++ IDE with the compiler integrated or just an IDE.
- With this IDE, we may use integrated debugging (using GDB). We can use the debugger to conduct all of the standard debugging actions on the source code.
- It contains a localization capability that allows it to work in a variety of languages. When we initially start the IDE once it has been installed, we can choose the language. We can also change the language using the settings at any moment.
- This IDE, like the others, includes an "Auto-Completion" feature for the code we write.
- It has a syntax highlighting editor that may be customized to make source code more understandable.
- It is possible to edit and compile resource files with this tool.
- There is a Tool Manager in the project that provides several tools that can be used.
- This IDE also includes Find and Replace functionality.

- We may construct various programs using the Dev-C++ IDE, including Windows, Console, Static libraries, and DLLs.
- To establish our project kinds, we can also construct our project templates.
- The Dev-C++ IDE may also be used to produce Makefiles, which manage the application's building process.
- It supports both the Class Browser and the Debug Variable Browser.
- A Project Manager oversees it.

Installation

Below is a step-by-step installation guide for Dev-C++.

- The first step in running the installation is to choose the language you want to use.
- After choosing the proper language, you will be prompted to accept the licensing agreement that appears.
- Following that, you must choose the components you want to install as part of the Dev-C++ installation. You are given a list of components that are available for installation and a tick next to each component. Each box can be checked or unchecked to indicate which components to install. Once all of the components have been chosen, click next.
- The installer now asks for the destination folder where the Dev-C++ files, libraries, and other files will be copied. Click Install after you have specified the destination folder location.

- When the installation is complete, a "finish" prompt appears, indicating that the installation is complete. After that, you may run the Dev-C++ IDE by clicking "Finish."

Sublime Text Editor

Sublime Text is a powerful text editor for programmers. You will adore the user interface's fluidity, as well as the incredible features and performance. Rather than waiting for online IDEs to compile and output your results, you can do it yourself. You can use Sublime to build and compile your program quickly.

Installation

- **Install Sublime Text Editor:** Download and install the Sublime Text Editor setup file from here.
- MinGW Compiler is a native Windows port of the GNU Compiler Collection (GCC) that includes freely distributable import libraries and header files for creating native Windows applications.
- Install all of MinGW's Basic Setup.
- Make a list of all the packages that need to be installed.
- Under the Installation tab, select the Apply Changes option.
- **Creating the Right Environment-** GCC is now up and running after you have completed the procedures above. The Path of the Environment Variable must be modified. To do so, follow the instructions below:

- Right-click on My Computer and select Properties > Advanced System Settings > Environment Variables.
- Look for path> on the System Variables Tab now. To create a new path, go to path> Edit > New.
- Now go to the C drive and look for the bin folder inside the MinGW installation folder.
- The path to the bin folder should be copied. The path is C: MinGWbin by default.
- Copy and paste the new route into the list, then click OK. Because the path variable has been adjusted, Sublime Text can now access g++ from its terminal.
- Create a file and name it CP.sublime-build

```
{
   "cmd": ["g++.exe", "-std=c++17", "${file}",
        "-o", "${file_base_name}.exe",
        "&&",
"${file_base_name}.exe<inputf.in>outputf.out"],
   "shell":true,
   "working_dir":"$file_path",
   "selector":"source.cpp"
}
```

- The preceding block of code is used to read data from the file "inputf.in" and print it to "outputf.out."
- **Creating a Window Layout-** Make three new files in the order described below, and make sure they are all in the same folder.
- file.CPP: The file in which the code is written.
- inputf.in: This is the file where the input will be given.
- outputf.out: The output will be presented in this file.

Execute the following actions now:
- Select View > Layout > Columns from the View menu. This will divide the workspace into three columns. Make three columns out of the three files.
- Select the build system we just built from Tools > Build System > CP by going to View > Groups > Max Columns.
- **Prepared to Run the Programs-** Precompile Headers: You can speed up the compilation process by precompiling all header files, including the bits/stdc++.h header file. To do so, take the following steps:
- Locate the stdc++.h header file. This file is located in "C:MinGWlibgccmingw326.3.0includec++mingw32bits" by default.
- On the current folder, open the Power shell or the command window. To do so, right-click while holding down the Shift key.
- To compile the header, use the command below.

    g++ -std = c++17 stdc++.h

1.4 C++ "Hello, World!" Program

Now, we will learn how to write a simple C++ program called "Hello World."

A "Hello, World!" program is a basic program that displays the phrase "Hello, World!" on the screen. Since it is such a basic program, it is frequently used to teach a new programming language to a beginner.

Let's have a look at how the C++ "Hello, World!" program operates.

First, Install the C++ editor on Your Computer if you have not already set up the setting to run C++ on your computer.

Keep in mind!
- To print output on the screen, we utilize std:cout.
- If we want to utilize std::cout, we must include iostream.
- The main() function is where the code is executed. This function is required. This is a perfectly good C++ application that does not do anything.

Let's start to write your first code.

C++'s Program "Hello World!" includes

// **Your First C++ Program**

Any line in C++ that begins with " // " is a comment. The purpose of comments is to help the person reading the code comprehend the program's operation. The C++ compiler completely disregards it.

#include <iostream>

The preprocessor directive #include is used to include files in our application. The contents of the **iostream** file are included in the above code.

This enables us to utilize cout to print output on the screen in our program.

For now, just remember that **#include** is required to utilize **cout**, which allows us to print output to the screen.

intmain() {-}

The main() function is required in any valid C++ program. The curly braces show where the function begins and ends.

This function is where code execution begins.

std::cout<<"Hello, World!"

The stuff inside the quotation marks is printed by std::cout. It has to be followed by and then the format string. The format string in our case is "Hello World!"

The "; " character denotes the conclusion or end of a statement.

Return 0;

The **return 0;** statement indicates the program's "Exit status." In layman's terms, the program comes to a close with this statement.

Now here is the complete Code:

```
// Your First C++ Program

#include <iostream>

int main() {
    std::cout << "Hello World!";
    return 0;
}
```

As an output of the above code, you will get the following result.

Hello World!

So, now you know how to write the basic C++ code. For better understanding, it changes the output statement with different words. You can practice the above code.

Chapter 2: Variables, Data Type, and Operator in C++

Data types, variables, and operators are the very basic concepts of C++. Some operators are considered as the basic building blocks of this high-level computer programming language. Usually, we use them to program our projects and to obtain the required results through their usage. Data types are the essential concept among these three concepts, and no one can understand C++ programming without having command over these three basic concepts.

Now, we will discuss some required variables, operators, and data types of C++ programming.

2.1 Variables of C++

In C++, variables serve as memory locations. They are just the name of the container or element containing the data or values needed later in the program for execution. It can be specified using a combination of characters and digits, or special symbols such as underscore(_), and data types such as char, int, float, and double. The first letter of the variables must begin with the letter alone except the reserved keyword.

In any programming language, variables are the most crucial component. Without a variable, any programming language is incomplete. We can also assert that the program cannot execute without variables. Variables are required for the C++ language to run, just as they are for any other programming language. Variables are used to store the value or string, not to run the program. The application will not run if no value is stored. As a result, variables are recognized as the programming language's backbone.

Variable Definition Rules and Regulations in the C++ Language

- Variables can be a combination of numerals, special characters such as and (&), underscore (_), or strings.
- Because C++ is a case-sensitive language, upper and lower cases are handled as separate variables. The variables educba and eduCBA will be addressed separately.
- Variables in C++ must begin with a character. The number will not be counted as the first character. 6educba is not an acceptable variable because it begins with a number, whereas educba6 starts with a character.
- Variables should not be used as a keyword in C++. The keywords used for this purpose include for, this, if, otherwise, while, do, char, this, and so on. In C++, some keywords cannot be used as variables.
- Variables must not contain any blank spaces. Edu cba is invalid because there is a space between edu and cba. However, educba or educba are both legitimate variables because the underscore sign is used to unite them.

In C++, how do you declare variables?

Before beginning the programs, variables might be declared. The following is the syntax for declaring a variable.

variable name data type; where

Datatype: It describes types of data that can be used to store value. Integers, chars, floats, doubles, short ints, and other data kinds are all possible.

Variable name: Defines the variable names. Except for the keyword, it could be anything.

1. int taxi, for example; 2. float 2.6, 8.3

For instance, int is a data type, while the cab is the name of a variable. We have specified two variables in the second example, where the float is a data type, and 2.6 and 8.3 are variables. The compiler has allocated storage for the variables once they have been declared, as it will be utilized for the program.

Illustration through Program

```cpp
#include<iostream>
using namespace std;
int main()
{
int x, y, z;
x = 10;
y = 3;
z = x + y;
cout << "Sum of two numbers is: " << z;
return 0;
}
```

2.2 Different Data Types in C++

The data type determines the type of data and the actions performed on ite. C++ includes a number of data kinds, each of which is represented in different ways in the computer's memory. Derived datatypes, Built-in data types, and user-defined data types are all available in C++.

Data types should be established prior to execution so that the compiler knows the type of data that certain variables contain. Only integer values can be stored in an integer data type; float or string values cannot be stored.

Built-in Data Types

Floating-point, integral, and void data types are the most basic (fundamental) data types given by C++. The floating-point and integral data types, in particular, could be preceded by a variety of type modifiers. So, these modifiers are keywords that change the data types' size, range, or may be both. There are long, short, signed, and sometimes unsigned modifiers. The modifiers are signed by default.

C++ ANSI has now introduced two new data types and bool, in addition to these basic data types. Let's see all built-in data types included in the C++ language.

Integer: Usually denoted by the letter "int." We can figure out how much RAM has been allocated. The integral datatype, which comprises the (character) char and (integer) int data types, is used to hold integers.

Characters: In the ASCII character set, characters are the alphabet, sometimes numbers, and also some other characters (like !, @,&, #, etc.). Because the characters are stored as an integer with values ranging from 128 to 127, the character data type is also considered as an integer data type in C++. 1 byte from memory is used by the char data type (that means, it can hold only a single character at once).

Floating-point: Real values such as 4.28, 74.7588765, 8.991, and -444.53 are stored using a floating-point data type. The double and float data types are included in this data type.

Void: The data type void is basically used to express an empty argument list for a function as well as the function's return type. When the void is basically used to mark or specify a null or empty list of parameters, it means the function will not accept any arguments, and when we use it as a return type, it means the function will not return anything or any value. No memory will assign to void; therefore, it cannot be able to store any value. As per the result, you cannot use void to declare a simple variable, but you may use it to declare a single generic pointer.

Bool: The bool data type can only carry Boolean values, i.e., true or the other one is false, with true representing one and false representing O. It simply requires one bit from the storage, yet it is kept in memory as a single integer. As a result, it will also regard as an integral type of data. The bool type of data is most typically used to represent the outcomes of a logical operation on data. It can also be used as the function's return type, indicating whether it is succeeded or failed.

Aside from the character data type, Language C++ also has the wchar-t data type, which is basically used to store or save 16-bit characters.

Derived Data Types

Derived data types are the data types that are derived from some built-in types of data. Arrays, junctions, references, and pointers are some of the derived data types supplied by C++.

Examples:

Array type: An array is basically a collection of elements of only the same type of data with the same names. Each element in the given array is accessible by a subscript value or unique index and is stored in contiguous (one after another) memory regions. The subscript value indicates the place of the element in the data type array.

Function type: A function basically is a self-contained program section that performs a single, well-explained task. Every program in C++ comprises of one or sometimes more functions that can be called from other portions of the program if necessary.

Reference: A variable's alternative name is referred to as a reference. In other terms, a reference is basically an alias for only a variable inside a program. A variable and its reference could be used alternately inside a program since they both refer to the same memory address. As a result, any modifications to one will have an impact on the other.

Pointer: A pointer is simply a variable that can be used to keep track of another variable's memory address. Pointers make it possible to utilize memory in a dynamic way. It is possible to allocate or de-allocate memory to variables at runtime with the use of pointers, which makes a program easier and efficient.

Data Types User Defined

Unions, structures, enumerations, and classes are some of the user-defined data types supported by C++.

Union, Structure, and Class: The most important features of the C programming language are union and structure. Union and structure allow you to arrange data types that are similar or distinct under a single identifier. However, in order to facilitate object-oriented programming, C++ had already extended the idea of union and structure by integrating certain new features and commands in the previous data types.

The class data type in C++ is a unique and newly introduced user-defined type of data that is the foundation of OOP. A class serves as a template for defining the data, information, and functions that go into a class's object. The keyword class is used to declare classes. The object of a class can be simply produced once it would be declared.

Enumeration type data: The enumeration data type is a collection of integer constants already named, defining all the possible values for enumeration variables. Enumerators are a collection of permitted values.

2.3 Operators in C++

With the help of examples, we will learn about the different kinds of operators in C++ in this tutorial. An operator in programming is a symbol that performs operations on a value or variable.

Symbols that execute operations on values and variables are known as operators. For instance, the addition operator + is used for adding the numbers or for addition, and the subtraction operator - is used for subtraction.

In C++, there are six different types of operators:

- Arithmetic Operators
- Assignment Operators
- Relational Operators
- Logical Operators
- Bitwise Operators
- Other Operators

Arithmetic Operators in C++

To conduct arithmetic operations on different variables and data, these operators are employed.

As an example,

X+Y;

The addition + operator is applied for combining two variables, named X and Y. In C++, there are various arithmetic operators.

For Example, Arithmetic Operators Code

```cpp
#include
using namespace std;

int main() {
   int a, b;
   a = 7;
   b = 2;

   // printing the sum of a and b
   cout << "a + b = " << (a + b) << endl;

   // printing the difference of a and b
   cout << "a - b = " << (a - b) << endl;

   // printing the product of a and b
   cout << "a * b = " << (a * b) << endl;

   // printing the division of a by b
   cout << "a / b = " << (a / b) << endl;

   // printing the modulo of a by b
   cout << "a % b = " << (a % b) << endl;

   return 0;
}
```

The output you will get...

```
a + b = 9
a - b = 5
a * b = 14
a / b = 3
a % b = 1
```

As we might assume, the operators +, -, and * compute addition, subtraction, and multiplication, respectively.

Increment and Decrement Operators

So, the C++ also has an increment and a decrement operator: ++ and -- respectively.

- ++ increases the value of the operand by 1
- -- decreases it by 1

For example,

intnum = 5;

// increment operator
++num; // 6

C++ Assignment Operators

To assign values to variables in C++, assignment operators are employed. As an example,

// assign 6 to b
b= 6;

Here, we are assigning a value of 6 to the variable b.

Here are all the assigning operators given below:

Operator	Example	Equivalent to
=	a = b;	a = b;
+=	a += b;	a = a + b;
-=	a -= b;	a = a - b;
*=	a *= b;	a = a * b;
/=	a /= b;	a = a / b;
%=	a %= b;	a = a % b;

Relational Operators in C++

To check the relationship between two operands, a relational operator is utilized. As an example,

This operator will check if the value of a is greater than b or not.

a > b;

So, here in this sentence > is a C++ relational operator. It will check if the value of a is greater than b or not.

If the relationship between this operator is true, it returns 1, but if it is false, it returns 0.

Here in this table, we have collected all the operators for your ease.

Operator	Meaning	Example
==	Is Equal To	3 == 5 gives us **false**
!=	Not Equal To	3 != 5 gives us **true**
>	Greater Than	3 > 5 gives us **false**
<	Less Than	3 < 5 gives us **true**
>=	Greater Than or Equal To	3 >= 5 give us **false**
<=	Less Than or Equal To	3 <= 5 gives us **true**

Logical Operators in C++

To determine whether an expression is true or false, logical operators are utilized. If the expression is true, it will return 1, but if it is false, it will return 0. In C++ language, logical operators were frequently used to make decisions.

Operator	Example	Meaning
&&	expression1 && expression2	Logical AND. True only if all the operands are true.
||	expression1 || expression2	Logical OR. True if at least one of the operands is true.
!	!expression	Logical NOT. True only if the operand is false.

Bitwise Operators in C++

Bitwise operators are used in C++ to execute operations on single bits. They're only compatible with char and int data types.

Here in this table, we have mentioned all the Bitwise operators.

Operator	Description
&	Binary AND
|	Binary OR
^	Binary XOR
~	Binary One's Complement
<<	Binary Shift Left
>>	Binary Shift Right

Chapter 3: Strings in C++

In this chapter, we are going to learn about Strings in C++. We will discuss how to use strings in your C++ program and the different types of strings utilized in the C++ program. So let's get started.

3.1 What is String?

The string is a C++ library function that aids in executing all string-related operations in the program. A string's data type is also allocated to a variable with a string of characters surrounded by double quotation marks. A String variable is any variable that has a continuous string of characters allocated to it. Let's look at how the String data type is used in the C++ programming language.

The string is one of the most used data types in the C++ libraries. A string is a variable that records a sequence or a list of letters or other characters, such as "Hye!" or "Your homework is due on June 10th!" To build a string, we must first declare it and then store a value, just like the other data types.

A String in C++ is simply a random sequence containing different characters defined within the C++'s defined library set.

C++ allows programmers to utilize strings to insert text wherever it is required. Strings could be reversed, joined, and supplied to a prior function, and so on.

We can also use C-styled strings in C++ since C code can be run on a C++ compiler.

The C++ string header <string> must be included at the top of the program in order to use the string data type. In addition, instead of requiring the onerous command std::string, you will need to use namespace std; to make the short name string visible. As an example,

std is a C++ namespace that contains a lot of the functionality found in C++.

C++ libraries are standard; you would not need to know anything else for the purposes of this lesson regarding **namespaces**. As a result, your program would contain the following #include's in it.

in order to take advantage of the string type

#include <string>

using the std namespace;

Basic Operation of String

Let's go into the details of the string manipulations you will be performing the most.

Counting the number of characters in a string.

In this feature of string, the number of characters included in that string are counted. The length method( ) returns the total amount of characters in a string, including punctuation and spaces. Length( ) is a member function, for many of the string operations, and we call member functions with dot notation. The recipient string is to the left of the dot, and the member function we are calling (e.g., str. length()) is to the right. We are seeking the length from the variable str in such an expression.example program:

```cpp
#include <string>
#include <iostream>
using namespace std;
#include "console.h"
int main() {
string small, large;
small = "I am short";
large = "I, friend, am a long and elaborate string indeed";
cout << "The short string is " << small.length()
  << " characters." << endl;
cout << The long string is " << large.length()
  << " characters." << endl;
return 0;
}
output:
The short string is 10 characters.
The long string is 48 characters.
```

Individual character access.

Using square brackets, you can access individual characters within a string as if it were a char array. Within string str, positions are numbered from 0 to str.length() - 1. [] can be used to read and to write characters within a string.

example program:

```
#include <string>
#include <iostream>
using namespace std;
#include "console.h"
int main() {
string test;
test = "I am Q the omnipot3nt";
char ch = test[5]; // ch is 'Q'
test[18] = 'e'; // we correct misspelling of omnipotent
cout << test << endl;
cout << "ch = " << ch << endl;
return 0;
}
output:
I am Q the omnipotent
ch = Q
```

Strings are passed, returned, and assigned.

When it comes to assignment, C++ strings are supposed to work like regular primitive types. A deep copy of the character sequence is created when one string is assigned to another.

/ makes a fresh duplicate of string str1 = "hello"; string str2 = str1;

str1[0] = 'y';/ just affects str1, not str2.

When you pass and return strings from functions, the string is cloned. Unless you explicitly pass the string by reference, changes to a string parameter within a function are not visible in the calling function.

Two strings are being compared.

The == and != operators can be used to compare two strings for equality. Assume you inquire about the user's name. The application prints a nice greeting if the user is Julie. The application displays the standard notice if the user is not Neal.

Finally, if the user is Neal, the answer is less enthusiastic.

Searching in a String

The string member function Find( ) is used to look for a certain string or character within a string. Str.find(key), for example, searches the receiver string str for the key.

A string or a character can be used as the parameter key. (We say the locate member function is overloaded since it can be used several times.) The constant **string::npos** indicates that the key is not found, and the return value is either the starting position where the key has been found or the constant string::npos, which indicates that the key has not been found.

You can choose to control which section of the string is examined on occasion, for example, to find a second occurrence after the first. There is an additional integer argument that can be used to find the occurrence.

Extracting Substring

Substrings are being extracted. You might want to remove bits of a larger string to make new strings. Substrings are created using the substrate member function from portions of the receiver string. The beginning position and the number of characters are both specified by you. For instance, str.substr(start, length) creates a new string containing characters from str beginning at position start and continuing for length characters.

This member function creates a new string with a duplicate of the characters supplied. Therefore, it has no effect on the receiver string.

Chapter 4: Array in C++

In any programming language, arrays are crucial. Instead of storing variables or a collection of a similar data type separately, they give a simpler approach of storing them together. The array's values will be accessed one at a time.

So, in this chapter, we will discuss the array completely and understand how to utilize an array in C++ code. The array is a crucial component in C++ since it aids memory management and increases the program's efficiency. Because of its ability to store multidimensional data, it can be employed in a variety of methods. When you need to store the same data type values, an array is always the best option. It not only saves resources but also shortens the time it takes for a program to run.

So let's learn how to use an array.

4.1 Introduction to Array

In C++, an array is a collection of comparable data types such as int, char, float, double, and others that are stored using the index value and can be accessed using simply the index value. It uses a single variable to store all of the instances of variables. In C++, an array can be defined in three ways: by specifying the array's size, directly initializing array elements, or specifying the array's size with its elements.

To allow data to be handled by any application, we must first enter the data into the application. This implies that the value should be saved somewhere in the application until the program executes.

The computer language provides a variable to fulfill the function of storing values. Variables are used to store values so that the application can use them to generate the anticipated result. As values are stored in variables, they take up space in the memory allocated to the application. As a result, the best coding strategy is to ensure that the variable is used as little as feasible. The concept of the array was created to address the memory allocation issue caused by the development of a large number of variables. The array can be thought of as a collection of values of the same datatype.

How do arrays work in C++?

The following is a description of how arrays work:

- The array's purpose is to store values of the same datatype. It is designed to work in the same way as the variable, and the only advantage it has over the variable is that it may hold many values at the same time. We must provide the number of variables we wish to store in the array while creating an array in C++ or any other programming language.
- It is worth noting that the array's size remains constant during the application's lifetime and cannot be altered dynamically. Once the array's size has been determined, we can store the same number of values in it. If the array's data type is set to an integer, it will not take any values that are not integers. The index will be used to locate the value held by the array.
- For example, if the array can hold two values, the second value will be stored at the array's one position

because the array's index starts with zero. We will learn how to create arrays in the future.

4.2 Types of Arrays in C++

Single Dimensional Arrays and Multidimensional Arrays are the two basic forms of variables in the C++ programming language. The single-dimensional array stores values in the form of a list, whereas the multidimensional array stores value in the form of a matrix. We will look at each of the types with an example.

Array with a Single Dimension

A single-dimensional array can be defined as a type of array that can carry the values of a single data center as a list. It is the most basic type of array because it requires little effort to define and initialize. It can be written as inta[10], where int denotes the data type and the array size. The sample below will help to clarify things.

Code for Practice

```cpp
#include <iostream>
#include <conio.h>
using namespace std;
void main()
{
int val_array[3];
int int_val=1,counter;
cout<<"Please enter three numbers that you want to multiply"<<endl;
for(counter=0;counter<3;counter++)
{
cin>>val_array[counter];
int_val = int_val*val_array[counter];
}
cout<<"The multiplication of these three numbers is = "<<int_val;
getch();
}
```

The program above is created to accept three inputs from the user, which are then processed to generate the multiplication value for all three. Valarray is the name of the array user, and the array can hold three values. The loop is used to take in the array's values, which were then multiplied. The intval variable has been used to store the result of the multiplication. The function will not return any value because it is void in nature.

Multidimensional Array

A multidimensional array is an array that stores values in the same way that a matrix does. The two-dimensional array is frequently used, and as the number of dimensions increases, the array becomes more difficult. Working with a two-dimensional array, for example, is much easier than working with a three-dimensional array. For each dimension of the two-dimensional array, two sizes must be defined. The two-dimensional array can be written asinta[5][3] in the program. The value will be stored in this array as a matrix with five rows and three columns. Let us look at an example to help us comprehend.

Code for Practice

```cpp
#include <iostream>
#include <conio.h>
using namespace std;
int main()
{
int val_array[5][5];
int count_rows,count_cols,counter1,counter2;
cout<<"Please enter the size of the rows and columns that you wnant to input: ";
cin>>count_rows>>count_cols;
cout<<"PLease enter the values for matrics in row wise manner"<<endl;
for(counter1=0;counter1<count_rows;counter1++)
for(counter2=0;counter2<count_cols;counter2++)
cin>>val_array[counter1][counter2];
cout<<"The matrix will be as follows"<<endl;
for(counter1=0;counter1<count_rows;counter1++)
{
for(counter2=0;counter2<count_cols;counter2++)
cout<<val_array[counter1][counter2]<<" ";
cout<<endl;
}
getch();
return 0;
}
```

We have utilized a two-dimensional array in our program. The array utilized is two-dimensional, according to the manner it has been defined using two sizes. The array would have been three-dimensional if there had been three sizes. The user is prompted to enter the desired number of rows and columns in the matrix. After the user has specified the numbers, they are prompted to enter the desired values in the matrix's rows and columns. The user has specified 2 3 in this case, indicating that the matrix should have two rows and three columns. They had to submit six values in the form of a matrix with two rows and three columns.

4.3 Creating and Passing an Array

How to Create an Array?

The following is an explanation of how to generate arrays in C++:

The method for creating the array is the same as that for creating variables. The declaration of the array is the initial step. We can either initialize the array at the same time as it is declared, or we can initialize it later. The data type of the array, the array's name, and its size must all be specified when defining the array. The syntax for declaring the array is simply shown below.

Datatype array_name[size];

Ex. intfirst_array[10];

This array can hold up to ten integer values. The array's name is the first array, and the number inside the huge bracket indicates the array's size. Let's look at how to declare and initialize the variable all at once.

Intfirst_array[4] = { 1,2,3,4}

Intfirst_array[]= {1,2,3,4,5,6}

We can see in the previous example that the array with the size four has accepted the four values. It will show an error if you try to submit more than four values. You can also store as much data as you like if you do not define the variable's size.

Methods of passing an Array

The following are examples of array passing methods:

To pass a variable as a parameter to any method, it has to receive the value from the datatype and the name of the variable that will retain the Value. The mechanism for passing the array to the method is the same as for passing any other variable. The only difference is that instead of specifying a single variable, we will have to use an array of a certain size in its place. Let's look at this in terms of syntax.

//defining method that accepts an array as a parameter.

inthandle_array(int a[6]);

handle_array is the name of the method, and it takes an array as a parameter. An array is designated by the letter a, and it can hold up to six values. Let's look at how the argument can be supplied to the handle array method.

intarrr[6] = {1,2,3,4,5,6};

handle_array(arr) ;

We must first assign the data to other variables before passing them to the handle array method. After the values have been assigned, we must call the handle array function with the array as an argument. The array has been assigned with the values and supplied as an argument to pass the values that the handle array function has been defined in the above snippet.

Chapter 5: C++ Pointers

Variables are regions in the computer's memory that can be accessed by their identifier, as detailed in earlier chapters. Pointer eliminates the need for the program to care about the physical address of the data in memory. Instead, it refers to the variable by its identifier.

A C++ application sees a computer's memory as a sequence of memory cells, each with its own location and size. Data representations larger than one byte can be stored in memory cells with neighboring addresses because these single-byte memory cells are structured in this fashion.

When any variable is called or declared, it is given a specified memory location in which we need to keep its memory address. C++ applications, in general, do not actively choose the addresses of memory where their variables are kept.

In this chapter, we will discuss, what pointers are, how pointers use memory, how variables are assigned to pointers, and so on.

5.1 What are Pointers?

A pointer is a variable whose value is another variable's address. A pointer, like any other variable or constant, must be declared before it can be used. A pointer variable declaration takes the following general form:

Type *var-name; Here, type denotes the pointer's base type, which must be a valid C++ type, and var-name denotes the pointer variable's name. The asterisk you use to declare a pointer is also the asterisk you use to multiply. On the other hand, the asterisk is used to indicate a variable as a pointer in this sentence.

C++ pointers are simple and enjoyable to learn. Some C++ activities are easier to complete with pointers, while others, such as dynamic memory allocation, are impossible to complete without them.

As you may be aware, each variable is a memory location, and each memory location has an address that can be accessed using the ampersand (&) operator, which denotes a memory address.

- Null Pointers- C++ provides null pointers, which are zero-valued constants defined in a number of standard libraries.
- Pointer Arithmetic- Pointers can be utilized with four different arithmetic operators: +, --, +, -++, --, +, -++, --, +, -++
- Pointers vs. Arrays- Pointers and arrays have a close relationship.
- An array of Pointers- Arrays can carry a large number of pointers.
- Pointer to Pointer- You can have a pointer on a pointer in C++, and so on.
- Passing Pointers to Functions- Passing an argument to a function by reference or by address allows the called

function to change the provided argument in the calling function.
- Return Pointer from Functions- A function in C++ can also return a pointer to a local variable, a static variable, or dynamically allocated memory.

5.2 Declaring Pointers in C++

Pointers Declaration

When a pointer points to a char, it has distinct properties than when it points to an int or a float since a pointer can directly refer to the value it points to. The type must be known after it has been dereferenced. To do so, a pointer's declaration must indicate the data type to which the pointer will point. The following syntax is used to declare pointers:

type*name

Above, type command denotes the data type to which the pointer points, this is the type of data that the pointer is going to point, not the type of the pointer itself.

int * number;

char * character;

double * decimals;

These are three-pointer declarations. Each one is supposed to point to a different data type, but they are all pointers, and they will probably all take up the same amount of memory space (the size in memory of a pointer depends on the platform where the program runs). However, the data they point to, does not take up the same amount of space or be of the same type: the first one points to an int, the second to a char, and the third to a double. Although these three sample variables are all pointers, they have distinct types depending on the type they point to int*, char*, and double*, respectively.

The asterisk (*) used to declare a pointer simply indicates that it is a pointer (it is part of its type compound specifier). It should not be confused with the dereference operator, which is likewise written with an asterisk (*). It is just two separate things represented by the same symbol.

Code for Practice

```cpp
// my first pointer
#include <iostream>
using namespace std;

int main ()
{
  int firstvalue, secondvalue;
  int * mypointer;

  mypointer = &firstvalue;
  *mypointer = 10;
  mypointer = &secondvalue;
  *mypointer = 20;
  cout << "firstvalue is " << firstvalue << '\n';
  cout << "secondvalue is " << secondvalue << '\n';
  return 0;
}
```

Output

firstvalue is 10
secondvalue is 20

Chapter 6: Control Statements and Loops

In a programming language, a control statement is used to control the program's flow. They are nothing more than a term or a set of statements used in a program to pass control to another statement based on certain conditions. It assesses the result and executes the necessary statements based on the supplied condition.

Control statements, also known as if statements, if-else statements, break statements, continue statements, for loops, while loops, and do-while loops, are statements that control the flow of a program in order to execute a piece of code. Some important control statements available in the C++ language will be discussed in this chapter.

6.1 Statements and Flow Control

A simple C++ statement is a program's individual instructions, such as the variable declarations and expressions discussed previously. Loops are always terminated by a semicolon (;), and they run in the same sequence as they occur in the program.

Programs, on the other hand, are not bound to a set of statements in sequential order. A program may repeat code portions or make decisions and bifurcate during its execution. C++ includes flow control statements for this purpose, which specify what our program must do, when it must do it, and under what conditions.

A generic (sub)statement is required in many flow control statements discussed in this section. This statement can be either a simple C++ statement or a compound statement, such as a single instruction followed by a semicolon (;). A compound statement is a collection of statements (each ending in a semicolon), all of which are grouped in a block and contained in curly braces: {}

The whole block is treated as a single statement (composed of multiple sub statements). When a generic statement appears in a flow control statement's syntax, it can be simple or compound.

6.2 Selection Statements:

if and else

If and only if a condition is met, the if keyword is used to execute a statement or block. Its syntax is as follows:

if condition statement is a statement that is used to determine whether something is present or not

The expression being evaluated is called condition in this case. The statement is executed if this condition is true. If it is false, the statement would not be executed (it will just be ignored), and the program will continue directly after the selection statement.

The code segment below, for example, prints the message (x is 100) only if the value stored in the x variable is 100:

```
if (x == 200)
cout<< "x is 200";
```

This sentence is disregarded if x is not exactly 100 and nothing is printed.

If you want more than one statement to be performed when the condition is met, wrap them in braces ({}), producing a block:

```
if (x == 200)
{
cout<< "x is ";
cout<< x;
}
```

By utilizing the otherwise keyword to offer an alternative statement, selection statements with if can also define what happens if the condition is not met. Its syntax is as follows:

If (condition) statement1 is true, then statement2 is true.

Statement1 is executed if the condition is true, and statement2 is executed if the condition is false.

With the goal of verifying a range of values, several if + else structures can be concatenated. Consider the following scenario:

```
if (x > 0)
cout<< "x is positive";
else if (x < 0)
cout<< "x is negative";
else
cout<< "x is 0";
```

By concatenating two if-else constructs, this prints whether x is positive, negative, or zero. Again, by combining the statements into blocks encased in braces, it would have been possible to execute more than one statement per case:

Switch Statement

The switch statement's syntax is a little strange. Its goal is to find a value among a set of potential constant expressions. It is like concatenating if-else statements, but it is only for constant expressions. The most common syntax is:

```
switch (expression)
{
  case constant1:
    group-of-statements-1;
    break;
  case constant2:
    group-of-statements-2;
    break;
  .
  .
  .
  default:
    default-group-of-statements
}
```

Switch analyzes expression and checks if it is equivalent to constant1; if it is, group-of-statements-1 is executed until the break statement is found. The software jumps to the end of the switch statement when it sees this break statement (the closing brace).

If the expression is not equal to constant1, it is compared to constant 2. If it equals this, group-of-statements-2 is executed until a break is discovered.

Finally, if the value of expression does not match any of the previously given constants (which might be any number), the program performs the statements that follow the default.

Because it employs labels instead of blocks, the switch statement has a strange syntax that dates back to the early days of C compilers. Break statements are required after each group of statements for a particular label in the most common application (see above). All statements after the case (including those under any other labels) are likewise executed until the end of the switch block, or a jump statement (such as break) is reached if the break is not specified.

It is preferable to use concatenations of if and if else statements to check for ranges or values that are not constant.

6.3 Iteration Statements (loops)

Loops repeat a sentence until a condition is met or a specified number of times. The keywords while, do, and for are used to introduce them.

The while loop

The while-loop is the most basic type of loop. Its syntax is as follows:

while (expression) condition

While the expression is true above, the while-loop simply repeats the sentence. If the expression is no longer true after any statement execution, the loop terminates, and the program continues after the loop. Consider the following example of a while-loop countdown:

```cpp
// custom countdown using while
#include <iostream>
using namespace std;

int main ()
{
  int n = 10;

  while (n>0) {
    cout << n << ", ";
    --n;
  }

  cout << "liftoff!\n";
}
```

In main, the first statement sets n to a value of 10. In the countdown, this is the first number. The while-loop then begins: if this value meets the condition n>0 (that n is greater than zero), the block after the condition is executed, and the process is continued as long as the condition (n>0) is true.

When using while-loops, keep in mind that the loop must conclude at some point. Therefore, the statement must change the values checked in the condition to compel it to become false at some point. Otherwise, the loop will keep looping indefinitely. The loop in this example includes −n, which reduces the value of the variable being evaluated in the condition (n) by one, making the condition (n>0) false after a specific number of loop iterations. To be more exact, after ten iterations, n equals 0, indicating that the condition is no longer true and the while-loop is terminated.

The do-while loop

The do-while loop is a loop in which you perform something while doing something else

The do-while loop, which has the following syntax:

while (condition) statement;

It behaves similarly to a while-loop, with the exception that the condition is evaluated after the statement rather than before the execution of the statement. While loop ensures that the statement is executed at least once, even if the condition is never met. The following example application, for example, repeats any text the user enters until the user says goodbye:

```cpp
// echo machine
#include <iostream>
#include <string>
using namespace std;

int main ()
{
  string str;
  do {
    cout << "Enter text: ";
    getline (cin,str);
    cout << "You entered: " << str << '\n';
  } while (str != "goodbye");
}
```

In the above program, when a statement runs at least once, such as when the condition to verify at the loop's end is specified within the loop statement itself, the do-while loop is frequently favored over the while loop. The user input within the block determines whether the loop finishes in the preceding example. As a result, even if the user wants to exit the loop as quickly as possible by typing goodbye, the block in the loop must be executed at least once to request input, and the condition can be determined only after it has been executed.

The for Loop

The for loop is made to iterate several times. Its syntax is as follows:

for (initialization; condition; increase) statement;

This loop, like the while-loop, repeats the statement while the condition is true. However, the For Loop also includes particular locations for initialization and an increment expression, which are run before the loop starts for the first time and after each iteration, respectively. As a result, using counter variables as a condition is particularly handy.

Here is an example of a countdown using a for loop:

```cpp
// countdown using a for loop
#include <iostream>
using namespace std;

int main ()
{
  for (int n=10; n>0; n--) {
    cout << n << ", ";
  }
  cout << "liftoff!\n";
}
```

In a for-loop, the first three fields are optional. They can be left blank. However, semicolon signals between them are necessary for all situations. For example, a loop without initialization or increase (equivalent to a while-loop) is for (;n10;++n); whereas a loop with the increase but no initialization is for (;n10;++n) (maybe because the variable was already initialized before the loop). A loop with no condition is the same as a loop with a true condition (i.e., an infinite loop).

Because each field is run at a different point in the loop's life cycle, it is possible to utilize more than one expression as an initialization, condition, or statement. Unfortunately, because these are simple expressions rather than statements, a block cannot be used to replace them. They can, however, employ the comma operator (,) as expressions: This operator is an expression separator, which means it can separate numerous expressions when only one is anticipated.

6.4 Jump Statements

Jump statements allow programmers to change the flow of a program by jumping to certain areas.

Break Statement

Even if the loop's end condition is not met, the break statement breaks the loop. It can be used to break an infinite loop or cause it to terminate sooner than it would otherwise. The C++ break statement is used to break loops and switch statements. In the specified state, it interrupts the program's current flow. Only an internal loop splits in the case of an inner loop.

The Continue Statement

The continue statement instructs the computer to skip the rest of the loop in the current iteration, as if the statement block's end had been reached, and jump to the beginning of the next iteration. For the loop to continue, the declaration C++ is used. The present program flow is maintained, and the remaining code is removed at a certain point. Only an inner loop continues if there is an inner loop.

The Goto Statement

Goto allows you to jump to a certain point in the program. This unconditional leap is unaffected by nesting levels and does not result in stack unwinding.

As a result, it is a feature to utilize cautiously, preferably within the same block of statements, especially if local variables are present.

Chapter 7: Function and Scope of Variable

With the help of examples, we will learn about the C++ function and function expressions in this chapter. Now we will study what a function is and what its parameters are. Let us go over what local and global variables are

So, let us get started!!!

7.1 C++ Function

In C++, a function is a collection of statements that receives input, processes it, and returns a result. The purpose of a function is to consolidate common tasks that are performed regularly. You will not write the same code twice if the inputs are different. Simply put, you will call the function with a different set of parameters.

The main() function is one of the functions found in every C++ application. Your code can be divided into distinct functions. Every function should perform a specific task as a result of this division.

The C++ standard library includes a large number of built-in functions. These functions can be called within your program.

What Does It Mean to Define a Function?

A function is a collection of statements that work together to accomplish a specific goal. It could be phrases that conduct routine operations or statements that perform specialized jobs like printing.

Functions can be used to simplify code by splitting it down into smaller components called functions. Another advantage of using functions is that it saves us from writing the same code again and over. We only need to write one function and then call it as needed, rather than writing the same set of lines over and over.

Calling a Function

When we have a function in our software, we need to call or invoke it based on the requirement. The function will only execute its set of statements to give the required results when it is called or invoked.

It is possible to call the function from anywhere in the program. If the software uses more than one function, it can be called from the primary function or any other function. The "Calling Function" is the function that calls another function.

The swap function is called the primary function in the above example of switching integers. As a result, the primary function is now the calling function.

7.2 Types of Functions in C++

There are two types of functions in C++, as indicated below.

Built-in Functions

Library functions are another name for built-in functions. These are the functions that C++ provides, so we do not have to write them. These routines can be used directly in our code.

These routines can be found in the C++ header files. For example, the headers <cmath> and< string> have built-in math and string functions, respectively.

Let's look at an example of a program that uses built-in functions.

```
#include <iostream>
#include <string>
using namespace std;

int main()
{
string name;
cout << "Enter the input string:";
getline (std::cin, name);
cout << "String entered: " << name << "!\n";
int size = name.size();
cout<<"Size of string : "<<size<<endl;
}
Output:

Enter the input string: Software Testing Help
String entered: Software Testing Help!
Size of string: 21
```

The headers <iostream> and <string> are used here. The <iostream> library defines data types and various input/output methods. The <string> header contains string functions like getline and size.

User-Defined Functions

Users of C++ can also define their own functions. These are the functions that the user has defined. The functions can be defined anywhere in the program and then called from anywhere in the code. Functions, like variables, must be declared before use.

Let us take a closer look at user-defined functions.

The following is the general syntax for user-defined functions (or simply functions):

return_typefunctionName(param1,param2,....param3)
{
Function body;
}

As a result, each function, as described above, has:

The value that functions return to the caller function after completing a task is known as the return type.
- functionName : A unique identifier for naming a function.
- List of parameters: In the above syntax, these parameters are denoted by param1, param2,...paramn. When a function call is made, these are the arguments that are provided to the function. We can have functions with no parameters because the parameter list is optional.

- A group of statements that perform a specified purpose is referred to as a function body.

As previously stated, we must first "declare" a function before utilizing it.

7.3 Function Declaration and Definition

Declaration of a Function

A function declaration informs the compiler about the function's return type, the number of parameters it uses, and the data types it uses. The declaration, which includes the names of the function's parameters, is optional. A function prototype is the same as a function declaration.

For your convenience, we have included several function declarations examples below.

Intsum(int, int);

The above declaration is for a sum function, which takes two integers as input and returns an integer value.

void swap(int, int);

This indicates that the swap function takes two int parameters and returns nothing. Hence the return type is void.

void display();

The function display has no parameters and returns no type.

Definition of a Function

A function definition contains everything that a function declaration does, plus the body of the function, which is surrounded in braces ().

Furthermore, it should contain named parameters. When a function is called, the program's control is passed to the function definition, executing the function code. When the function's execution is complete, control returns to the place where the function was called.

The following is the definition of the swap function for the above declaration:

void swap(int a, int b){

    b = a + b;

    a = b - a;

    b = b - a;

}

It is worth noting that a function's declaration and definition can occur at the same time. There is no need for a separate declaration if we declare a function before referencing it.

We can see that there is a function swap in the preceding example that takes two int parameters and returns nothing. It has a void return type. We have not declared this function individually because it was defined before main as a calling function.

We read two integers in the primary function and then call the swap function by giving them two integers. The two integers are switched using conventional logic in the swap function, and the swapped values are reported.

7.4 Scope of Variables

The scope of anything can be described as the extent to which it can be worked with. The variable's scope is also defined in programming as the amount of program code within which the variable can be accessed, declared, or interacted with. Variable scopes are divided into two categories:

- Global Variables
- Local Variables

A scope is a section of a program, and there are three areas where variables can be declared in general.

- Local variables are variables that exist within a function or a block.
- Formal parameters are used in the definition of function parameters.
- Global variables are variables that exist outside of all functions.

Local Variables

Local variables are the variables that are declared within a function or block. They can only be utilized by statements that are included within that function or code block. Functions outside of their own are unaware of local variables. The following is an example of how to use local variables.

```cpp
#include <iostream>
using namespace std;

int main () {
    // Local variable declaration:
    int a, b;
    int c;

    // actual initialization
    a = 10;
    b = 20;
    c = a + b;

    cout << c;

    return 0;
}
```

Global Variables

Global variables are defined at the beginning of the program, outside of all functions. The value of the global variables will remain constant over the life of your program.

Any function has access to a global variable. That is, once a global variable is declared, it is available for use throughout your whole program. The following is an example of how to use global and local variables.

```cpp
#include <iostream>
using namespace std;

// Global variable declaration:
int g;

int main () {
    // Local variable declaration:
    int a, b;

    // actual initialization
    a = 10;
    b = 20;
    g = a + b;

    cout << g;

    return 0;
}
```

Use these programs for practice because practice will make your learning perfect.

Chapter 8: Class and Objects in C++

In this chapter, we will learn about objects and classes and how to utilize them in C++ with the help of examples.

We studied functions and variables in an earlier chapter. It is sometimes preferable to group together relevant functions and data to be more logical and easier to work with.

Assume we need to compute the area and volume of a rectangular room based on its length, breadth, and height.

We can use three variables, such as length, width, and height, as well as the functions, calculate area() and calculate volume() to complete this work ().

Instead of defining distinct variables and functions in C++, we can wrap these related data and functions in a single location (by creating objects). Object-oriented programming is the name for this programming paradigm.

However, before we can build and use objects in C++, we must first understand classes.

8.1 C++ Class

In C++, a class is the fundamental building block of Object-Oriented programming. It is a user-defined data type with its own set of data members and member functions that can be accessed and used by establishing a class instance. A C++ class is similar to an object's blueprint.

Consider the following scenario: Consider the Automobile Class. There may be many automobiles with different names and brands, but they will all have some essential characteristics, such as four wheels, a speed limit, and mileage range. Car is the class here, and wheels, speed limitations, and mileage are the attributes.

- A Class is a data type that has data members and member functions that the user defines.
- Data members are data variables, and member functions are the functions that control these variables; these data members and member functions together define the properties and behavior of the objects in a Class.
- The data members in the previous example of class Car will be speed limit, mileage, and member functions will apply brakes, increase speed, and so on.
- The sole difference between a class and a structure in C++ is that a class defaults to private access control, whereas a structure defaults to public.
- All of OOPS' features revolve around C++ classes. Inheritance, encapsulation, abstraction, and other concepts are discussed.
- Separate copies of data members are stored in class objects. We can make as many class objects as we need.
- Classes have additional qualities, such as the ability to build abstract and immutable classes, which we shall cover later.

For example, all birds in the class of birds can fly and have wings and beaks. So, in this case, flying is a habit, and wings and beaks are features. Moreover, while there are many distinct birds in this class, all of them share the same behavior and traits.

Similarly, a class is nothing more than a blueprint that declares and defines traits and behavior, such as data members and member functions. These characteristics and behaviors will be shared by all objects in this class.

Creating a Class

In C++, a class is defined by using the keyword class and then the name of the class.

The curly brackets define the class's body, which is followed by a semicolon at the end.

```cpp
class Room {
    public:
        double length;
        double breadth;
        double height;

        double calculateArea(){
            return length * breadth;
        }

        double calculateVolume(){
            return length * breadth * height;
        }

};
```

We created a class called Room in this section.

Data members are the variables length, breadth, and height defined within the class. Also recognized as member functions of a class are the functions calculateArea() and calculateVolume().

8.2 C++ Object

A Class's instance is an Object. When a class is defined, no memory is allocated; nevertheless, memory is allocated when instantiated (when an object is formed).

The term "class" refers to a blueprint or a template. When we define a class, no storage is assigned. Objects are instances of a class, which contain the data variables stated in the class, and on which the member functions operate. There are multiple data variables for each object. Constructors are special class functions that are used to initialize objects. Constructors will be discussed later.

When the object is no longer in scope, another particular class member function called Destructor is invoked to free the memory that the object has reserved. Unlike JAVA, C++ does not have an automatic garbage collector; instead, the Destructor fulfils this function.

When a class is defined, it just defines the object's specifications; no memory or storage is allocated.

We need to build objects in order to use the data and access functionalities defined in the class.

```
// sample function
void sampleFunction() {
    // create objects
    Room room1, room2;
}

int main(){
    // create objects
    Room room3, room4;
}
```

In the sample function, two objects of the Room class, room1, and room2, are generated (). In the same way, the objects room3 and room4 are created in the main menu ().

As can be shown, we can create objects of a class in any program function. A class's objects can also be created within the class or in other classes.

A single class can also be used to produce an unlimited number of objects.

8.3 Concepts of C++ Object-Oriented Programming

C++ programming's main goal is to introduce the concept of object orientation to the C programming language.

Inheritance, data binding, polymorphism, and other notions are all part of the Object-Oriented Programming paradigm.

True object-oriented programming is a programming paradigm in which everything is represented as an object. Smalltalk is widely regarded as the world's first object-oriented programming language.

OOPs (Object Oriented Programming System)

A real-world entity, such as a pen, chair, or table, is an object. Object-Oriented Programming (OOP) is a programming methodology or paradigm that uses classes and objects to create a program. It provides various notions that simplify software development and maintenance:

- Object
- Class
- Abstraction
- Encapsulation
- Inheritance
- Polymorphism

Object

The term "object" refers to any entity that has a state and behavior. For example, a chair, a pen, a table, a keyboard, a bicycle, and so on. It might be both physical and logical in nature.

Class

The term "class" refers to a group of items. It is a logical thing.

Inheritance

Inheritance occurs when one object inherits all of the characteristics and behaviors of its parent object. It allows for code reuse. It is utilized to achieve polymorphism at runtime.

Polymorphism

Polymorphism occurs when a task is accomplished in multiple ways. For instance, to persuade the buyer in a different way, draw something, such as a form of a rectangle. To implement polymorphism in C++, we employ Function overloading and Function overriding.

Abstraction

Abstraction is the process of concealing internal features while displaying functionality. For example, we do not know how a phone call is processed within.

To achieve abstraction in C++, we employ abstract classes and interfaces.

Encapsulation

Encapsulation is the process of combining (or encapsulating) code and data into a single entity. For instance, a capsule is wrapped in many drugs.

OOPs, have an advantage over procedural programming languages.

- OOPs, simplify development and maintenance, whereas Procedure-oriented programming languages are difficult to handle as projects expand in size.
- Data concealing is provided by OOPs, whereas global data can be accessed from anywhere in a Procedure-oriented programming language.
- OOPs significantly improve the ability to imitate real-world events. If we use the Object-Oriented Programming language, we may propose a solution to a real-world problem.

Conclusion

Learning to code is analogous to learning any language or, more precisely, a family of languages in many ways. All scripts must follow a set of underlying rules. In addition, each script has its own set of regulations.

It is hardly an exaggeration to say that coding is the DNA of the modern world. Coding is required to run any website, phone app, computer software, and even a few kitchen appliances. This is why programmers are so essential in defining the digital era and the future.

For the people interested in a career in computer science, new markets are opening up. Aside from the obvious examples of physicists, IT personnel, designers and artists, engineers, and data analysts, opportunities in manufacturing and finance are beginning to emerge. This means that coders are in high demand and are typically financially well compensated.

This book will help you become familiar with coding, which you can convert into a lucrative job or even an enjoyable hobby if you so desire. Even if you do not plan to work in the field, knowing how to code is impressive and extremely valuable. It will be seen favorably. You will not only be prioritized as a job candidate, but you will also be able to interact successfully with your team.

C++ is a strong, expressive programming language for beginners that is simple to pick up and use. However, books about learning C++ programming can be dismal, grey, and uninteresting, which are no fun for anyone. That is why in this book, I have crafted interesting ways to learn C++ programming, which makes learning fun.

C++ breathes life into Core programming and introduces you (and your parents) to the world of easy C programming. This book will walk you through the fundamentals while you play with innovative (and often humorous) sample programs, which helps you in practicing your learning. New words are defined, code is colored, dissected, and explained, and full-color pictures make things light-hearted.

Programming tasks in the last few chapters will stretch your mind and improve your understanding. You will have developed three to four entire games by the end of the book.

I hope after reading this book, you have learned how to do the following when you begin your programming journey:

- Make use of basic data structures.
- Using functions and modules, you may organize and reuse your code.
- Control structures such as loops and conditional expressions can be used.
- Classes and objects.
- OOPs, concept, and its benefits.

So, should all the enjoyment be reserved for serious adults?

This book is your passport to the wonderful world of computer programming. But for becoming a perfect programmer, I strongly advise you to practice and practice utilizing the information in this book. I am confident that you will become a skilled coder.

And do not forget to share your feedback about this book. Leave a review on Amazon if you have enjoyed this book and found it useful in your coding journey.

www.ingramcontent.com/pod-product-compliance
Lightning Source LLC
Chambersburg PA
CBHW071422070526
44578CB00003B/657